WHEN BROWN skin was Beautiful

a collection

John Robert Bland

Printed in the United States of America

First Printing, 2016 Twitter: JRBland_Author

TABLE OF CONTENTS

What Is the deal with the anthem? I have been harassed at work as instigators would put little flags on my computer and go hide to see how I would react. I would toss them, only because it was being used to incite conflict. That is how you respond to bullies. It is no different from sexual harassment. Harassment is harassment. We were raised on the flag, even when we did not know what it meant. Every morning we pledge allegiance. That was the order, and nobody cared to explain why. Thirty black kids in a third grade classroom in the sixties standing at the white teacher's order to pledge allegiance. She do not want to take questions, because kids can be brutally honest. "So teacher, if that is the way it is, why can't my father find a job, and why he had to leave us so mama can apply for AFDC?" Father cannot get a job because he is the wrong color, so we are were between a rock and another rock with flood waters at our ankles. We did not wear the flag as a shirt or a hair cover. Okay, now that I think about it, maybe if daddy had draped himself with the flag before applying for jobs, we may have been hired, or beaten to death. Black soldiers returning from WWI and WWII (my father) were beaten and often killed for walking around the United States wearing their uniforms after fighting in wars, with no jobs waiting. Business as usual, and so what, you know your place; fall in. The flag has nothing to do with going to war and dying, as many men did. When I was tracked down while attending college in good standing during the Vietnam War, the draft board did not give me a speech about the flag and fighting for your freedom. No, they were abrasive and ordered me to get down to take a physical. I had to go to the president of the college to save myself. They were straight up gangsters. I do not think, for a second, that while you are on the verge of possible getting killed in battle, that you are thinking about the flag. "Hey private, we forgot the flag, Its back in the bunker that was bombed. You go back to see if you can find it," "go to hell captain". That is how that would have gone down in Vietnam by white, black, brown, red, and yellow. Of course, I was not sitting at the table when the flag or the constitution were decided among. I was probably wiping the table clean after it went down. So what do you expect from me, anymore than what I have given, which has been far beyond the respect I have received. So leave me alone when I kneel and pray for you.

TAKE A KNEE

Most who make their money
exploiting all those they can
and even those not aware
would be shocked by the trail

When you get that cash
at who expense it was
Do not forsake our struggle
our history
Kneel down and take a knee
Kneel down and take a knee
Kneel down and take a knee
Kneel down and take a knee

Poor people are at the bottom
to help rise others to the top
They way it has always been
and that will never never stop

The question is the sharing
No one should without food or home
Those who are that greedy
they move the needle to dead wrong

When you get that cash
at who expense it was
Do not forsake our struggle
our history
Kneel down and take a knee
Kneel down and take a knee
Kneel down and take a knee
Kneel down and take a knee

That could be old cotton money
that pays you for scoring a touch down
from which so many died so inhumane
and you should kneel and pray in shame

to be accountable for life today
every thing is connected to the game

When you get that cash
at who expense it was
Do not forsake our struggle
our history
Kneel down and take a knee
Kneel down and take a knee
Kneel down and take a knee
Kneel down and take a knee

The owners keep on keeping on
Finding a way to gamble what they stole
Reason the so wide between rich and poor
400 years of free labor facts untold

When you get that cash
at who expense it was
Do not forsake history
Kneel down and take a knee
Kneel down and take a knee
Kneel down and take a knee
Kneel down and take a knee

Pray to Jesus on your knees
Heavenly Father help us please

Pray to Jesus on your knees
Heavenly Father help us please

Sandy

My beautiful flower girl
I miss you Sandy
When I could not find you
and they acted like you were fine
but you were suffering
in the streets
and if you stay out there too long
you are just as well as dead

I imagined finding you
approaching and asking
if you know who I am
It has been many years
You would stare at me clueless
This is Uncle John

It hurts me why people give up on family
Why they turned backs on you
and one day I asked
and had to sit
because they said you were dead
I miss my beautiful flower girl

Interment

I grew up in housing projects
an internment camp
where we were stacked
on top of each other
to keep us in one place
so we could be observed
so we could be restricted
so we could be managed
We had great teachers
but we were caged
plus most of us were poor
Now you could be poor and still learn
but if you are caged and restricted
It mess with your mind

Doctor Stereo

The doctor said
we have a pill that works well
on your people.

And what people is that
Doctor?

African Americans she said

You mean to tell me you all
made a pill just for African Americans?

Yes

Well no thank you and by the way Doctor,
you appear to be comfortable with that
expression of racism.

You are mistaken

No, you are. I never
introduced myself as an African American.

Thank you and goodbye.

WHEN BROWN SKIN WAS BEAUTIFUL

Can you remember
when the streets were fun
Nowadays when mentioned
it's about time to run
When kids had names
you could spell
and you rarely heard news
of a neighbor's son in jail
When we had our focus
on moving up
rather than lacking self esteem
and being abrupt
And you could count on your brother
having your back
instead of hating you so much
with guns waiting to attack
and when all was said and done
with no money to buy anything else
When brown skin was so much
beautiful all my itself

Full Course

A well planned meal
as her love is the napkin
that comes with the meal
After sipping her soup
of small talk
the main course her problems
and if you appear to clear your plate
she will bring in the family
because grandmother need
medicine
and sis need school fees
while you eat her dessert
After the meal you will pay
the bill
It is best not to sit for the meal
but many can not resist
the napkin

Quiet Love

I enjoy love that is quiet
without cellphones
a third party
checking in like a girlfriend
wanting to share

I enjoy love that is quiet
without the mention
of financial needs
to leave something
on your mind for morning

I enjoy love that is quiet
without the mention
of anything
except the sound
of hearts beating
between a warm embrace

You are just dreaming bro

Spy

I see affection and I spied
to see how it works
and maybe I will be inspired
to discover a first

So many do not know
how to love
they pretend
So I spy to understand passion
an obsession
that never ends

Trump Rally

Those people who attend
this man's hate sessions
reacting like ugly humans
who drags us backward
as a nation
They must return home
to shower off that hate
and look at themselves
to say
what was I thinking?

because you would like to think
they were raised better

Danger

I am so anxious to write this piece
because I am filled with anger
that so many people do not care
that we are in clear and present danger
Police are driven by stereotypes
that our media aggressively promote
That law enforcement have procedures
allowing the police to partake
in tactics that take lives
and where commonsense is always late
The stereotype and the police
will always be a mismatch
while corporation use agents to stir the pot
and iPhones to carry the bad news

Suva Fiji Islands Stroll

farewell
to running into Merwyn
on Thompson Street
reminiscing our basketball days
made us both feel young
he passed last year and so sad
on my way to Marks Street
to drop in on old friend Henry
always comments on my fitness
but he stays home now
leaving me a stranger in the shop
and feeling unfit
the lone recognizable street hawker
left over from back in the day
when he was a young fellow
now silvered haired
wearing a nice bula shirt
was all smiles
Mela and Steve still there
the old shop at bridge crossing
nothing has changed
not even the furniture
I hope they never retire
running into one of the
old basketball girls at MHs
bad news that Marita passed
and please no more of this
Kenny's big smile
from the hair saloon
which is no longer his
but he is there
stopped in on Ravin
who has done very well
with his fast food business
and he is still the race car champ
turned back to see Simi
a friend for life
but Viti and mum

they may have immigrated
no where in site
and a natural instinct
to stop at Traps to yell at Gary
but he left us too soon
RIP
as the vibe had changed
but there is a Tora sighting
the old school DJ
and sit down for a meal at
Mary's Cottage
but it has a new owner
so keep on moving
Ken is hard to catch at Dragon
while Victor left us quietly
and maybe I will catch Mawi
playing his guitar
at the Holiday Inn tonite
always nice to see my brother
and I heard from Tomasi
my bball teammate
back then with Boston
and terrible news
Solo had his leg removed
diabetes got him
YMCA Joe died last year
and then Michael just left us
jovial Iliesa
an icon who I watched
complain to Travelodge Hotel
back in the day
for refusing Fijians use of the restroom
he did not have to
but his heart did
so, I lament in all the sadness
while hanging on to the few
joyful moments
the smiles
the smiles
Isa Lei

Caging Children

Brown children subjected
to being caged
by the ugly Americans
who live in rage
They stole from those
who they build walls around
to cover their guilt
so obvious and profound
And anyone should be caged
they are those who hold us back
The worst of humanity
as love and respect they lack

Mother's Solution

Be they black
white
brown or red
skinheads
crips
ASW or MSG
Sitting in those cells
dating those four walls
for life
They all reminisce
about their mothers
the care
the food
the love
and while a moment of
bad judgement
maybe have ended freedom
they hold on to
their mothers
therapy that the system
refuse to acknowledge
because it will keep them out
It will work

Pain and Death

I remember my mother
taking me to Cook County
because I had pain
but once I got around
those white jackets
feeling no pain

So I stood on the corner
where I grew up long ago
where teens had been killed
trying to distinguish pain
from dead and gone
and fro my vantage point
pain hurts more

3 In My Life

In my life
I have been invited to
3 weddings
including my own
all Chinese
figure that

In my life
I have been the recipient
3 moving violations
deserving none
but that shit happens
all the time

In my life
I have attended
3 funerals
someone bought a big knife
to the last one
and so excuse me

In my life
three things yet to accomplish
catch a fish
drive a manual
tie my shoes properly
they are not important

Past Notice

All of our black leaders
those who dared to speak out
Justice and equality
the world over
are either dead
by assassination
or shut down
until you return to work
Do not run when it
gets tough

Losing Juanita

If my mama knew
or if she was alive
when my sister was found dead
she would have had a fit
It would have taken
every ounce of my strength
to keep her upright
mama do not like losing
anything

pancakes

pancakes are innocent
as I can have them alone
on my plate
no animal parts staring
and hugging nearby
only a soft brown cake
filling my expectations
alone
as life should be

My Brothers and Sisters

I hope my brothers
my sisters
by different mothers
same father
I hope my brothers
my sisters
understand generations
that we must not take it
for granted
I hope my brothers
and sisters
seize the moment
rather than having
the moment
seize them
I hope my brothers
and sisters
will love each other
I hope

SUPERMAN PREZ

Tired of economic blues
without a living wage
Trying to feed your family
feel locked inside a cage
In spite of useless Washington
who trade progress for hate

Looking like true losers
while the president pulls the weight
Once in a lifetime leader
with vision that is truly rare
Teaching this world to grow up now
because Obama really cares

So a lesson in tolerance
whether the haters liked it or not
As the people re-elected
the prez who refuses to stop
Once in a lifetime leader
adored throughout the land
Voted by majority voters
for change we all demand

Maybe he didn't do everything
but we as the people are to blame
To allow progress to sit and wait
held hostage by a gang
Let this be a lesson yes
if you are serious about change
Help the ones full of hate
to get off that ship of shame

What is wrong with healthy people
and without it you are going to die
So commonsense should tell you
carry my brother over stealing the pie

that respectful
he said he would
But given the obstacles
he did the best he could
Those who disgraced us
forever tagged with shame
To refuse the will of the people
changing every rule in the game

All you haters
what have you done to improve this place
Besides holding on to a legacy
to divide the human race

Superman prez
breaking down barriers
like no one before
Superman prez
In spite of those dividers
opened up some doors

regrets

somebody is going to jail
like taxes it never fails
goodbye to freedom they knew
as they learn the meaning of blue

once black men feared for life
white men hung them out of spite
young man buried without grave stone
as families never planned on

Go Girl

these girls will sit and listen
to all your problems
and agree all the way
occasionally slapping your thigh
like a play book
she will not disrupt the flow
to get compensated
playing ignorant to innocence
as he speaks broken English
and she knows the hook is in
speaking Tagalog to the waitress
he don't have any clue
he goes on giving the briefing
the US compared to the Philippines
like they don't have television
like she doesn't have relatives there
and she has heard it all before
but she possesses the patience
of a psychiatrist
to hear his aches and pains
comfort him in any way
as he is having the time of his life
like Columbus discovering
what has already been discovered
but he will leave
and he will pay
if she hasn't already led him to the ATM
yes he will and yes she will
Go girl!

Solutions

I see problems
that have solutions
but some people resist
It is as if they received
a call after midnight
to resist change
because change will change
change
and we can not have
any of that change
and so we return to
talking about the problem
that requires a change

Maurice Clarett

the program will promote you
use you
until there is nothing left
and if you still have legs
you can move on
if not
you are disposable
left for the dead

(Former Ohio State football standout who net worth is only
$15,000, according to Wikipedia)

hinges

you can not call out the police
if you are not protecting
your village

doors wide open to collect rain
mold on the breathe
of some

destined to wear orange or die
leaving children
lonely and confused

and once the hinges are off
nothing but debris
will touch your soul

Coffeeville

You could be something
if you can dream some
and not just for yourself
but for everyone
Those who believed in you
and came out to vote
but also for others
who have given up hope

Those who are in shock
because times have changed
Let them find their way
or things will be just the same
Go beyond limits set before you
when minds were so small
Take a bite from the Apple
and do miraculous things for all

Sacrifice

Girls go on to college
to dawn hats and gowns
Degrees to go to work
for which some can be found
On the other hand
and so very sad to admit
that boys are to immolate
gangsters
who are scheduled to fail
and just waste away

Blue Line

walking thru that tunnel
to get the blue line

passing
humans

they seem barely alive

some asking for coins
others looking for heat

while holding my breathe
to avoid the urine stench

fellowship

standing around the dinner table
holding hands
not something I have participated
in a very long time
as one individual gives a speech
blessing the food and the occasion
as I felt my hand embraced firmly
but at times shaking
and I focused so much on that
than the blessing
maybe I need to do this more often
to endear the touch
and the power of touch by a stranger
in pure kindness

Baltimore hood

like vultures they wait
for the last wave to come
that will clear the path
the signal no more culture
gone forever never to return
where the jewels will be kept
and vacant lots developed
till you would never know
they were there
Play ball!

Beat Down

if it was just a beat down
the violence would be less
the energy to fight
takes the steam away
from embarrassing displays
but shooting with guns
so easy to conceal
so easy to fire
taking life with a flash
Never thought I would say
I miss those beat downs

Oh Shooting

oh
was that shooting last week
seem longer
but it wasn't that long ago
when the other one
and how we forget when people
are killed
to prepare ourselves for the next
shooting
because we care
but only when we are led to
and then we go back to forgetting
oh
was that shooting last week
and few are listening

weaves and dye

they grow up beautiful
and that rough around the edges
is attitude
and no need to touch that
but the miseducation starts
to turn innocent into fools
with imagination of white
and white woman they don't say
it is not right
if black women are not going
to put up a fight
rather they just let it ride
as sisters show up looking like
imitation of what I am talking about
from blonde hair to green eyes
sold out but that is the process
in fine print is the magnitude
so the mind can go numb
losing all that natural crown
and that other stuff
I call attitude

Pulitzer Prize

is disguised
reserved for the other
guys
that the judges' appetite
patronize
to not see beyond
what others idealize
and for a fee to play
for which can be criticized
but why not be specific
rather than generalize
or is it a brand name scam
to decriminalize
the Pulitzer Prize

Kudos

All about simple gratification
and somewhere along the way
somebody decided to use drug
to satisfy that gratification
or else there would be many upon many
of young smart black men and women
many graduates of traditional black colleges
because proud parents would demand it
inspired by the civil rights movement
and the legacy of Reverend King
and other role models in all professions
like professional black baseball players
the way it use to be
filling the entire Ebony Magazine
but the jobs for these proud young black men
would not be forthcoming
because the struggle for equality
the major impediment
and so we were marching and protesting
and many would die
but it was a worthy struggle
but somebody decided to shut down hope
and the quest for equality
by throwing cheap addictive drugs
into our equation
so that the community would self inflict its death
and cease its dedication to unity
the greatest threat to the system
that was losing its grip on shutting us out
because we were strong and smart
and they cut off the potential of our youth
each a leader to be reckon with
and to disrespect our traditional institutions
leaving them dangling to survive
and to disrespect elders
our civil rights movement

leaving us earmarked for prison cells
and so we turned on each other
the nearest and most innocent
while the chosen ones are giving wealth
but also given ignorance and selfishness
to turn their backs on us
while we kill each other
like those who really hate us
and it seem to be working
so well

Line in the Sand

they say
they can look beyond
beyond the color of his skin
because he will be
a great president

they say
they can look beyond
beyond his immoral behavior
because he will be
a great president

they say
they say these things
because they see an opening
to be the greedy
immoral Americans

Tariffs

China please go ahead with your tariffs
as they will not bother me
I will still be low waged or no wage
and still eating grits and lunch meat
Much like most of your people
as we are squeeze between this game
orchestrated by the rich on both sides
but you can do me a favor
include those hair weaves
those oversized trousers and tees
and that ridiculous jewelry
you pollute our poor neighborhood
causing many of our youth to die
Maybe we can break the habit
A blessing in disguise
China please go ahead
and don't forget us

Terrible Soul

when this terrible man
is finished
discarded by the climbers
who have no use for him
he will sit alone
and by his side black people
the same he hated
cut their housing
their healthcare
their vote
their freedom
but nevertheless
there holding bibles
comforting his bad deeds
trying to save his wretched soul

That Poison

knowing what you know
you should find the strength
find enough to be fearless
to declare war on your space
to those who distribute drugs
otherwise blind you are
forgetting our shiny stars
wasted and destroyed
so that those with poison
can please their masters
to destroy the beautiful unity
we once had

My King Jar

Our neighborhood was never the same
after they killed Martin Luther King
No event has exceeded the fear of that day
and so all of this over losing a leader
my young mind was trying to process
who had been pouring hope into my empty jar

Mama only had to say it once
"Do not leave this house or else"
as I watched Sam running and yelling out an obscenity
after dropping the bottle of whiskey he was hiding

So, with the fires from up on Madison Street
sirens
looting
curfews
police
national guard
and the memory of army tanks cruising
down our street
We were in prison

The aftermath was shocking and depressing
with no psychologist for us
and it stayed that way
Our neighborhood was never the same
and my jar still unfulfilled

Tattoos

getting one is just like
buying a new car
the novelty diminishes
shortly after the start

but many of you
can only afford to buy one
with only one space to park
one and done

until somebody tells you
they like your tat
so you get another one
to try to top that

it only starts a habit
for which you cannot control
keeping up with others
as you now focus on your toes

and when both visible
and unseen parking spaces gone
you now resemble
a no parking zone

Shame Antidote

Addiction of denial
wearing so much makeup
but the swelling is clear

Like ice cream to a child
crying uncontrollably
after craving a knee

Call them heroes
from the same toolbox
because it always seem to work

So by committee the guns
can be protected
much like molesters are

We Have Made It

They got on the train
dressed

He stood in a light colored suit
that was back in the day
would have been much too small
and would surely burst
at the seams

She managed to find a seat
wearing dress so eloquent
with all the amenities
to accent and she was beautiful
and turned heads

He was preoccupied with nothing
except calming her down
because he could see
he should have taken a taxis
as all eyes were on them

While she constantly boasted
so we could hear
that she was struggling with
the Aussie accent to replace
the Indian one she owned

Tasteless

While the media keep on
digging a hole
in our membranes
like tasteless Coke
to justify the behavior
of this man
that we shall accept
he is breaking new ground
All a lie

There is no new ground
just look around
People are homeless
next to so much dishonesty

There is no new ground
media
We are now being dragged
through the mud
So the rich can take
whatever ground
we are standing upon

Black Star

The few exceptions
they are so complicit
in some scheme
to keep us occupied
to enhance their riches
and if they prosper
then the white folks more
telling us we all can make it
is just another folklore
and when we raise our voices
to cry out with inequality and despair
they pull out the exceptions
you know them
to return us back to that cage of hell

12 Months My My

January
The beginning of a new horizon
trying to put mess behind
to get on a positive real
clinging to the same old vine
Mama calling everybody
in Chicago and down south
wishing everybody Happy New Years
while the trend have cast some doubt

February
Cold and trying to stay warm
as bills start piling on the bills itself
No use trying to pretend
that new car is not drowning yourself
Holiday cheers has a shirt life
just like people doing crack
When will you stop showing off
when you do not get anything back

March
The sun shines my way
a feeling of warmth and hope
to let me sit and think
about the condition have eloped
A welcomed moment indeed
as I hold my breathe within
to get my priorities in order
before the world turns on me again

April
I can see flowers blooming
in Mrs Johnson's front yard
Such a beautiful thing to behold
amidst despair's entourage
I wished all I could ever see
beautiful flowers to set me free
but soon I will hear the violence
and I will return to hiding inside of me

May
As I am trying to keep my mind
on things I have to take care
I am distracted by all this news
so depressing I get out of my chair
Then the phone rings
and somebody giving me the news
There is just no way in this world
to get out of the bad news loop

June
Summer and kids will be graduating
to what I ponder in pain
I pray not to this stock we see
not amounting to a thing
Join the military to fight
rich people driven wars
If you did not prepare for college
you will never close those other doors

July
killings are in full stride
as all the bad are on the streets
like there is something about carnage
and this summer Chicago heat
Never a quiet evening
followed by the morning news
while grave diggers complaining
of those back pain blues

August
Phone keeping ringing
while I'm trying to cook my greens
I can not be bothered
but it rings rings rings
So I answer the phone
to nothing but screams
Another nephew murdered
Now where did I put my crying tears cream

September
Go down to Cook County jail
to visit my grandsons
while some folks visit colleges
mines will graduate ex-cons
I got more sitting in jail cells
just rotting themselves away
than I have with good futures
got to be a better way

October
The month of my birthday
but there is nothing to celebrate
Do not wish me nothing
but pray this mess will go away
My bible is running out of blank pages
trying to keep up with those we lost
Got more of us buried
than those who own a house

November
They are running for office again
promising the same old lies
They own the playbook on us lawd
like a priest who sins
Nobody wants to stop the killings
instead they want more guns on the streets
This here black brown homicide
has become a business hard to beat

December
No break from violence
even when snow is knee deep
and temperature near freezing
but stuff still happening in these streets
There is no Santa Claus for sure
No way in this neighborhood
Only the Jehovah Witness
They are as fearless as cottonwood

Putting On Martin's Shoes

we have come a long way
from the freedom we had
across the rough sea waters
many died in chains so sad

too strong like rhythm to forget
our voices sing out our pain
we are still on a journey
to get back freedom from which we came

so that is why I am standing
and ready to go
I'm putting on Martin's shoes
because the struggle is not over no no

so that's why I am standing
and ready to go
I'm putting on Martin's shoes
because the struggle is not over no no

I say
I'm putting on Martin's shoes
because the struggle is not over no no

some say look to the future
so tell me which way is that
because no matter where I turn
suffering is what I am looking at

so that's why I am standing
and ready to go
I'm putting on Martin's shoes
because the struggle is not over no no
so that's why I am standing
and ready to go
I'm putting on Martin's shoes
because the struggle is not over no no

I say
I'm putting on Martin's shoes
because the struggle is not over no no

so that's why I am standing
and ready to go
I'm putting on Martin's shoes
because the struggle is not over no no

so that's why I am standing
and ready to go
I'm putting on Martin's shoes
because the struggle is not over no no

I say
I'm putting on Martin's shoes
because the struggle is not over no no

walk with me

I say
I'm putting on Martin's shoes
because the struggle is not over no no

we can make a difference

putting on Martin's shoes
putting on Martin's shoes
putting on Martin's shoes

Trending Helpless

Children
just stop by here
just open my door

Children
I am always waiting
to hear footsteps on my floor

to sit down and talk
because I want to know
to wash my dishes
because arthritis hurt so
to take out my trash
because stairs are slippery
to stop by to give me a hug
because I often feel lonely

Children
excuse my selfish pride
will not ask you too

Children
treat me with love and care
the way I raised you

Symbols of Hate

take down those statues
a record of hate
today is not too soon
one hundred years late
to hang on to hatred
to keep it alive
outsiders so arrogant
on native land
how long they have survived

Nina Simone

Ms. Simone had a first floor condo at the Franklin Towers off LaBrea and Franklin next door to my old friend from the Chicago Westside, also Roland, who still lives and manages the complex. During a visit from Fiji I once complimented Ms. Simone on her clothing that was both colorful and ethnic. She motioned her head and then she "you can go now".

She did not like Roland's wife at all, who is a ver fair skin blonde mixed with German, Native American and black blood. She despised her so much that one evening she turned on a water hose and place it on Roland's patio and let it run until it was noticed the next morning. Ms. Simone was nothing to play with, and I heard Ms. Simone was not so fond of light skinned women.

Threshold

stranglehold of law
allows wiggle room for injustice
like the slack
in a hanging rope
allowing the body to dangle
and not by chance
but intentionally crafted
to separate the haves
from the have not
in case the have nots
get in the way
of injustice

Hometown Beat Down

Police planted the seed
when I was three
That is when it became
very clear to me
Watching the Chicago police
beat up black men
My eyes wide opened
and my feet frozen
To make it painfully clear
who was in charged
To stay in your place boy
or we come down hard
I grew up fearing
white men wearing blue
Saw even in my dreams
what they will do
When black men were allowed
to wear the uniform blue
They had to prove they could beat
down black people too
So it came to be
blue against the black community
But back then we joined hands
in brother and sister unity
Elders never told us
to respect the police
Can you blame them
being harassed thank you please
So City fathers hated to see
the power when we unite
and began to create problems
to divide and make us fight
They killed our leaders
or they bought them out
to open the door for drugs
for guns to be distributed about
We had no jobs or a factory

to make our own grits
How do you jump from that
to killing each other carried no logic
Created revenues from violences
and even through our deaths
for which they are still riding
until nothing of us is left
Easier to sit back
and watch us kill ourselves
than to beat us down
as I witnessed myself
Now we have a glory mess
convoluted and disconjugated
black people to take the fall
when all of this is disseminated

Cicely Tyson

Ms. Tyson
is one of those longevity
sisters
like a Lena Horne
and the likes
who grace us with
all the reasons
to love our blackness
Good genes
for healthy living
Knocking down barriers
to achieve happiness
A black man's
syllabus
on why he needs to
pick up his game
on uniting
and get beyond
petty selfishness

Pretenders

When you have stolen something
and hurt so bad with guilt
you use a good book to hide
in a room with others like

You call yourselves believers
because you are in denial's den
of what you really are
and the hurt you have inflicted

So you call yourself a religion
and meet with others on Sundays
to pretend you are righteous
but come Monday
Tuesday Wednesday Thursday
Friday and Saturday
you make a fool out of Sunday

A GRADE FOR LIFE

Why are we so afraid to give every child an "A"
rather than occupy space so the school get paid
while the child just rots away

To teach each child because it will define their world
and demanding parents to grow up themselves
and protect their precious pearls

Starting with the ABCs and arithmetic they need
walking away with calculus and physics
and honors all up and down their sleeves

Rapping have had its day now go away
because we have lost so many trying to emulate
allowing community and progress to slip away

The ones you call and label not too bright
which means they hold everybody else back
and this is sounding so familiar i.e. civil rights

Every single day every child should leave with an "A"
and all the dysfunctional parents better recognized
to get on board because that is the only way

As if we are clueless where they will go without
a third grade reading level wearing a pair of Nike
hungry corporations already out there to take them out

And prisons waiting with arms spread so ever wide
like the first day of college on the other side
to steal another generation while we just go for the ride

Why are there more who want to tell us we can't
than those who dare to take the chance
forgetting many died to give your pathetic self a chance
Forced Feed

Just give us the metrics
and tell us
who is winning the war
Not overseas
I am speaking of
Rather the people next door

Will the children be safe
walking to and from
our schools
or is the neighborhood
still being operated
by these damn fools

You are either
winning or losing
those are the rules
Speak up
I can't hear you
and that is not cool

Constitution

Sorry to burst your bubble
now that you are comfortable
but the constitution was drawn
to protect those who were vulnerable

Certainly not the Native Americans
the people of the land
but clearly the European thieves
who still show their dirty hands

So they enacted laws
so others would not come alone and do
the immoral unforgiving acts
that they performed that are so true

To leave a place god planted you
to occupied and develop
to invade another's people place
greed that will not earn you god's feather

To carve it up so meticulous
so all at the table can eat until they get fat
and bringing over black people from Africa
to further show how sinful sin can get

So these families at the table
they called inhumanity a democracy
and even made a flag
to reinforce the hypocrisy

Church Divide

We do not worship together
and not many are saying a word
while ministers and priests
they preach the word so
that you would think
if you turned around
to face worshipers surround
that you would see a rainbow
like the real world we live
but it is all a lie
as they say
using god's name in vain
and if you think we have
turned the corner
that we are Christians of love
and people of faith
that prayers have been answered
You are so naive

Taken Aback

We live in a society of denial.
We go off to war and kill people,
yet we pray to go to heaven.
What kind of heaven could
that be?
Black people have
suffered through slavery,
reconstruction, and it goes
on an on while many seen to
be addicted to amnesia.
However, they recall
the Civil War and all the other
wars, so much that they called it history
and taught it in every school.
When slavery comes around it is brief
or they call it Black Studies
where the majority of the students
are black, because black studies
may not look good on the transcript.
This has gone on so long
that even black people either
do not know or have forgotten
about their history.

Taken Aback Too

We have the KKK to remind us
of the organized lynching in
which white men and their sons
took part in. Needless to say,
some of the killers are still
alive this very day. They use
to celebrate the torching of
a black man. With white shirts
and tie, they would assemble, and
not just the criminal deviates that
one would associate these inhumane
and unforgivable acts, they included
the mayor, police chief, the shopkeeper,
an even the church minister.
We have dirt poor black people and
filthy rich white people, and who
dares to explain it.
There is little wonder why many
whites would want to forget about
this chapter in their heritage.
What kind of heaven awaits such people?
Black people try to run away
from their pass. Some tell us this is
America and look at me, if I can make
it, you can too, but they are also
in denial. It is a numbers game,
and no university is going to accept
every black student from local high schools
who apply.

CHILD'S ADMISSION

Sorry Ms Mary for breaking your window
and calling you Crazy Mary
Obviously I was the crazy one

Sorry third grade girl
for hitting you in the face with snowball
That taught me to never hit a girl again

Sorry friend's uncle
stealing that one hundred dollar bill
from the top of your drawer
for which I bought a pant and shirt
but friend came by and asked for it back
Thought I was going to jail

That is all I have to be sorry for
right now as the day is still early

If I can find the part of you
that speaks for all
then maybe I can convince you
that there is no reason to stall
as love comes in bundles
and needs special care
or it will sit there all alone
with nothing to share

CTA

Chicago Transit Authority
I remember you well
Rode you throughout high school
and what stories I can tell
From those cold winter mornings
waiting for you to show up
Just before my feet would go numb
and my lips frozen shut
To those spring and summer days
when you were always right on time
Like during that daytime robbery
hiding behind you eased my mind
You took me to places
that I had never been before
Including some places
no welcome mat in front of the door
I can not remember one of your drivers
because they were not so user nice
I just got on and paid my fare
and joined others like sticky rice
All and all Chicago Transit Authority
you served my needs
To the extent that I have survived to reminisce
so thank you please

MOTHERHOOD

Mother will fight for their babies
They will even die
So if you think that badge
with privilege you
to violate that code
you are not only sadly mistaken
but you will face the fire of
motherhood

STUART SCOTT

Stuart
where you at man?
Your presence is missed
on that ESPN
Your bright personality
always made my day
A break from all the head games
in life I have to play
You brought a unique style
that melted both young and old
From a platform of sports
you were down right cold
Your cliches were hip
so much that they stuck
You changed the industry
like Kareem did with the hook
I will be honest dude
it didn't matter the color of your skin
You see you had evolved
into an international godsend
And your cancer
for which your courage overshadowed
Brought strength to countless
and above all that really mattered
Stuart things will never be the same
without your face around here bro
As cool as the other side of the pillow
your words and appropriately so

GOOGLE BACK

I discovered the wonderful Google Map
to take me back in my lifetime
to places that are forever fresh in my mind
A reunion of feelings that made me feel so fine

Curtis the tall one and Jasper too
and not to forget James the shy one who
lost his little brother Lewis not so long ago
out with his good friends to ease the blues

Bus fare got us on the Lake Street line
headed east for at least two miles
Going downtown were the money piles
Each a window seat and a grinning smile

Slow down bus driver man there's no hurry
We need to enjoy every single moment
No rush in us to get back to low rent
Taking a break from that high rise cement

Different kind of noises and yellow cabs
Every turn there is another high rise
Men wearing ties and women high heels
Step for step we move studying their eyes

Over to Michigan and Randolph Street
where the old library use to be
Some Ebonys and Jets we had to see
and a big old toilet where we all could pee

Then off to run all over Grant Park
where the big fountain sprinkled our skin
and confirming to each other right there and then
that we will most definitely visit that fountain again

Watch the cars as we crossed Lake Shore Drive
to the museum that had all kind of neat stuff to see
Animals' names we could not pronounce properly
as we went our own way to discover our individuality

We never budgeted for something to eat
but we managed each a chocolate donut yummy
So much for our bus fare back home you see
but an easy choice to make to please the tummy

Hey James found a quarter in the street
and we spent it on a bottle of Cold fizzling pop
Each of us taking turns under a counting clock
before James had the honor of drinking the last drop

After crossing Wacker Drive on Randolph
No tall buildings and few people to see
The produce market on both sides of the street
and a place that employed our neighbor Ms Marie

At Halsted Street looking for something else to see
so we walk over to Madison where it got creepy
A skid row of drunken and hopeless men so dirty
As we walked closely together to eyeball cautiously

Final sprint down to the Chicago Stadium up on Woods
and those smiles we left with that morning returned
but with hunger in our stomach we had properly earned
Walking proudly toward the projects with the stuff we had learned

So through this phenomenon Google Earth
I was able to go back nearly fifty years
without taking a single step I travelled far and near
to refresh good memories that were so vividly clear

AS I WAS SAYING

You know
this is the most wonderful part of a new love
you know that
so I will not spoil it by talking about it
anticipation
when you smell my skin and I smell your
before we even touch
and then comes the electricity
from our touching
gently
and the shivering from head to toe
and then
when we hold each other
in warm embrace
first it will like time have stopped
and when our bodies locked into each other
it will be the greatest feeling
and neither of us will want to let go
and that will be the start
of something special

Close Call

upset that my friend Big Mac
had a gun put in his face
not an easy thing to get over
as your heart starts to race
I can attest how abnormal
this shit really is to life
After living in the Fiji Islands
where guns are nowhere in sight
Murders by gunshots
as remote as can be
There you only see them
on US video a and movies
Of I saw some mess
turned my stomach upside down
I guess there is poison everywhere
the bad seed just goes around
Spousal beatings in Fiji public
was the ugliest I have seen
but nothing and absolutely nothing
to compare with this US killing

VIETNAM MOTHER'S CRY

Vietnam mother's cry
echoed across housing project high rise
Sharing the pain of a mother's loss
suddenly we became one big house

Embracing the moment of sorrow's path
forever entwined but we sometimes forget that
And while a son who feels like me in mama's eyes
left one day with a suitcase and an uncertain goodbye

Did not die on an unforgiving city street
by the police or from the choke of poverty
But rather from a war that we knew nothing about
killing people with names like Tran and Chau

Who looked nothing like rednecks down south
or the racists up north who shut us out
Poor child out there confused and all alone
trying to survive to get back home

Mississippi Chicago next stop Vietnam
the only job he could get goddamn!
Cemented in our minds to illustrate
forever stuck between a rock and a hard place

So as mama wiped her tears into her hands
over a war she could not comprehend
And no sooner we get over saying goodbye
there goes another Vietnam mother's cry

Death Car

my aunt had a death car
she didn't know it no worries
but the used car had a past
I can not tell you the story

when I went for a ride with. her
chest tighten and loss my breathe
struggled to get out
but never told my aunt no less

several months later
I noticed my aunt looking down
but no one was talking
as I asked around

then I looked at the car
and knew the reason why
was slowly killing my aunt
because that spirit would not die

Pot

Try to climb out
of the melting pot
You see
I am a potato
so I can't see the top
I might have to
step on some carrots
along the way
It is not that I want to
but what can I say
And if I get out
I will try with all
my might
to push that pot over
to make things right

Hustle

Will there be hackers
outside of the gate of heaven
selling last minute tickets to get in
Looking all official
Will you run into
one of the Fiji sword sellers
who speaks multiple languages
and can carve your name
into a wooden sword in seconds
Will there be standing room
and a VIP booth for those characters
who had their congregations
buy private jets
Will they wave at you to day
I told you so
Please Jesus
dont let it be true

Quiet Worry

Sometimes too quiet
without sounds of people yelling
because they do in my neighborhood
Poor people more than others
Space so tight
and like friction causing combustion
explosion
But I am not hearing that
and if I did
I would also hear fast moving cars
sirens
and my brother stopping by
to fill in mama
but it is so quiet
that I am worried

Ivy League

Corporations continue to
take our brightest
and they are using powerful stuff
They go off to Harvard
and they don't come back
Caught in the ivy
and the next time you see them
they are talking like fools

White for One Day

If I were white for a day
I would rush downtown
before anything opens
to get myself a line of credit
and just for the hell of it
maybe several
I would walk up to the curb
and laugh at the sight
of some Pakistani cab driver
breaking his neck to get my fare
while some well dressed black man
stands near fuming
and inform the brother that I
feel his pain
and that I will be walking

If I were white for a day
I might even get myself a desk job
not that I need one
or even have the qualifications
but I will take one anyway
because I know somebody
who know somebody else
and because I am white
I would leave at lunch time
and inform human resources
that I decided to take
a sabbatical
and mail the checks home please

If I were white for a day
I would talk to other white folks
about black people
because that's what they do
when they are not around
and I would take
in a basketball game

to watch a bunch of them
coach by a white man
run up and down the floor
with such athleticism
and would imagine what they do
to those white women sitting behind
but that is okay
as long as they are entertaining
and spending their money in communities
other than their own
and that Eddie cracks me up
and Michael is awesome too
but I think he is white

If I were white for a day
I would be trying to live forever
vitamins guns wan doo
and with so many privileges
that I would be looking over my shoulders
scared and running and hoping
that some nigger don't get mad enough
to take me out
so that the devil
can ship my ass off to hell
priority express

Diploma Overdue

High school diplomas
with that walk across the stage
subjected to sharecropping
for below minimum wage

Let those still living
who were subject to discrimination
to have their opportunity
for a once in a lifetime celebration

And let that be a lesson
that no man women child be exploited
so that those who share greed
can be privileged to being rewarded

Diet

We are not new to violence
It has always been a staple
in our diet
They gunned down Tuna
She was only 14
I was 15
They gunned down Wonder
She was 13
Kids having to see
Kids of neighbors
die in the streets
What a terrible diet we were served

Kids Deserve Better

He is that kid
The one who is a loner
The one who is a bully
teachers have no time for
or they just send them home
but the single parent want him out
Out of her sight to do her thing for 8 hours
and the first to say my child did it is so wrong
They want attention
The coach has his favorites
The teachers geared toward easy
Kids who listen and are headache free
They have their own drama waiting at home
Kid finds the gun
He needs to show it off
So that he is as popular with others
He takes that gun to school in his bag
He is embarrassed for the shoes he is wearing
He pulls out the gun and shoots it hitting whoever

All because he got no attention
All because some kids are poorer than others
even when they all are poor
All because his mother has no time for him
All because the system is set up for the likeables
All because adults are too lazy and now would
rather have armed police so they can return
to their comfort zone
While parents are ready to sue somebody to buy
stuff to be popular among peers
just like their son with the gun

FIGHT IN US

My people
can find a fight
in anything

If the old man dies
they will argue
over who will
collect the
insurance money

If a man gets drunk
from drinking Gordon Gin
somebody will argue
that he can drink
a whole pint
without getting drunk

If somebody
has a stroke
they will argue
over who stroke
was the worst

My people
dammit
can find
a fight in anything

Night Scare

How do you protect yourself
from a procedure
a procedure that can take
your life
All over a misunderstanding
on some evening night

In my car and on my way
to the other side of town
Watch the speed limit
speed traps here all around.
They will stop you for sure
nothing better to do
Make you sweat bullets
to try to make a fool out of you

Brother getting harassed again
Just for being a brother then
Brother out here all alone
I wish this brother was back at home

Got to keep my cool
and watch my hands
nighttime is not my friend
They will shoot you
in a second
and that's the way your life will end

Border Talk

countries so developed
so attractive
at the expense
of immigrants
but a glass of white wine
forget about the guilt
low wages
without benefits
Hollywood Hills Brentwood
Mexican laborers
picked up like hookers
from freeway exits
but a glass of wine
will make it better

Mr. James Smith, College Graduate

Why they call you
Bonecrusher?
He said because he used to
hurt people
That got my attention
have not ever hurt anyone
We were about similar
in age
Everything on him
was large
Former heavyweight champion
of the world
James "Bonecrusher" Smith
Once in the limelight
and sent into retirement
by a much smaller Mike Tyson
Can only imagine this giant
falling to the canvas as he sits here
Fallen from a stroke
humbled warrior
yet so intelligent
outclassing his knockouts
An author
Shaw College North Carolina
Bachelor in Business Administration
prominently exposed
that media found irrelevant
is hurting people
who would have expected
otherwise
from this 1975 college graduate

Just One Less Fool

I have been running
all of my life
chasing a dream
with no sunlight

Sometimes I smelled it
so I kept going on
I have not found it
but I am not returning home

You were always there
to push me to the ground
I am not going to get anywhere
as long as you are around

If I knew you were going there
I rather stay down here
Just one less fool
I swear

If I knew you were going there
I rather stay down here
Just one less fool
I swear

I can not figure out
why god placed you here
Must be a lesson to the struggling
to overcome all fears

You were always there
to push me to the ground
I am not going to get anywhere
as long as you are around

If I knew you were going there
I rather stay down here
Just one less fool

I swear

If I knew you were going there
I rather stay down here
Just one less fool
I swear

Words can not express
what I think about you
I could have enjoyed my life
were it not for you

If I knew you were going there
I rather stay down here
Just one less fool
I swear

If I knew you were going there
I rather stay down here
Just one less fool
I swear

Flag

Kindergarten kids pledge
allegiance to the flag
black kids remember the words
the song
white kids return home
to receive clarification
black kids grow up with it
second nature
white kids grow up using it
as a race
a privilege

Westside Scam

one two punch
all it really is
to remove my people
from the Westside
first they threw out
government vouchers
for a suburb ride
so that those folks
they move back yes
to the new Westside
two the drugs and guns
to kill and jail
most of all the rest
funeral and lawyer cost
will bring them to their knees
losing their property at best

and nobody is in a hurry
because it has been
a great success

Madison and Kedzie

from the school I watched
a small flame from a house
and people came out
with little children in panic
as I stood there frozen
with fear in my heart
beating like a bass drum
and the fames grew larger
to match those who stared
as there was nothing else to do
for the wooden house
a tinder box
melted before my eyes
and I realized
how instantly everything you own
can vanish
and prayed they all got out
because the once house
was now rubble
that the wind could toy with
and now comes the fire engine
to the black neighborhood

This Here President

A man who needs to return
to his box
for continuing education
A threat to mankind world over

Forget about stepping across
the aisle
Stop playing with fire
Time to step across town
Have lunch with others
Share experiences
Tear down the hatred

Football coaches
who coach black player
Merchants who sale goods
to people of color
Teachers who teach
school children
Holding on to deep prejudice

To sacrifice the environment
this man needs to go away
and be a lesson to us all
of what a human should not
grow up to be
Just that simple

Texas

I do not like Texas
because it is belongs to Mexicans
but I love the country
taken away by force
killing countless of. them
and now they celebrate
the carnage
a victory for those who killed
and name cities for them
while incarcerating so many
Mexicans and blacks
while they have conditioned
many to have pride
in how it came to be
people have the capacity
to fall in love with aroma
without regards to the ingredients
that some call patriotic
which sounds better than thieves

Sandra Bland

Sandra
on her way to start a new life
Stopped by the police
on some irrelevant mess
in the broader scheme of things
Arrested and jailed
and who knows what happened
but she died

There is a claustrophobia
That goes along with being stopped
It heightens when you are handicapped
and taken away
for something so minor
Placed in a cell
A place so foreign and enough
to make your heart stop

Sitting Window

Once Mama retired
the window became her job
Sit there throughout the day
humming favorite gospel hymns
waiting for anything
Knew neighbors' business
Evening comes along
she is there for the shift
with lights turned off
taking in every movement
A speeding police car
would be a bonus
to entertain possibilities
as curiosity peaks
until eyes grow weary
to signal time to punch out
Off to bed to rest
for the morning shift

Uncle's Warning

He said
"Don't you bury me in Chicago,
I aint playing with you.

I told him
"Uncle James, you know how
they are when you're gone.
They will throw you in the
nearest hole and party all
night."

He said
"Don't listen to what I want and
I will come back and get you.
I swear I will. Don't bury me in
Chicago".

Juanita

Sister Juanita
sad to say
one of the 500th
Chicago homicides to date
Just too horrific Mr. Mayor
to comprehend
As if somebody left the door opened
to allow death in
I am not sleeping well
until this carnage stops
Until you land grabbers
are exposed and sentenced
to rot

EXCUSE ME LORD

Have always be taught
to love my fellow man
and woman
and god knows that
much pretending
and I will accept the criticism
but pardon me
for not having an ounce of love
for former governor of Alabama
George Wallace
and the now sitting president
Donald Trump
and when his term is over
I will kneel with tears of joy
to have the rest of my life
free of hate from the top

Chicago Disconnect

You can meet some older brother
working security
at some downtown hotel
Retired policeman who lost his wife
Brother will share his life with you
An unforgettable and rare experience
to cherish

You can walk up to a counter
vaguely recognize the person next to you
until the light in your brain switches on
Wow
this is Marcus Murphy
one of my best friends in high school
over thirty years ago
and he is still wearing those coke bottle glasses
but he acts like he doesn't even know me

You can fly into a Chicago airport
without being able to get one relative
to pick you up
to stay at their place
in the place you were raised
everybody has an excuse
no time
no transportation
no job
no nothing
while they want to know
what are you going to do for them
which never stops

I skip them all to go downtown to listen
to the old brother tell me about his life
He has time for me

Reporting Lord

as if some dogs,
if that is how that wish
to be described,
got caught at the gates
and had to stay back
with humans,
and now faced with being
different in some ways,
depended on compassion
of the humans,
so very unpredictable
ranging from love to hate,
to accept them as they are
so that they can enjoy life,
and oh so familiar

did you know about this lord?

Misery Company

There are those
within your reach
who are addictive to no good
They want to be your friend
to influence you
and when they go sliding down
disgracing humanity
Well then
they want you to be their friend
to join them in their sin

3rd Year College

I woke up one morning
on that beautiful campus
to get myself in order
I had become a man
No longer flipping pages
but rather appreciating each word
that I missed out on earlier
when I was tossed over 11 schools
over 12 years
and that is where it began
an awakening
athletics to my waist side
I started on a journey that has not stopped

Disenfranchised

boys
they talk about
not the distant future
because vision is blind
no
they recant
what they saw
deaf to adult ears
and nothing new about that
so they feed off peers
what the police did
the guns they took
how they got away
and who got caught
as this game is the only one
until they are caught
by the game
the prisons
All without vision
as adults are too much
into themselves

BROWN ELEMENTARY KISS

first grade teacher
I guess she was nice to me
after all
I went on to second grade
you see

and so just maybe
but not forgetting
the only thing I remembered well
when she ask me to help
take papers to her car
it made me feel swell

and when I finished
that kiss so wet on my lips
unexpected no doubt
I quickly wiped it away
as I held my breathe
until I got out
of sight

but if I had told mama
you had better call the police

LA Curse

Los Angeles can be a cold place
to be so hot
Behind that veneer
is a struggle that never stopped
Both black and brown people
from all over
who were not greeted kindly
after they were discovered
Prohibit from crossing Wilshire
that is right
The other poor people who
got the treatment too were whites
They stole it from the Mexicans
didn't you know?
Then they tried to dictate where
people of color could not go

PLAYGROUND

When I was a child
we use to swing on that swing
until the blood rushed to our heads
too dizzy to swing anymore

We use to slid down that slid
until our little dirty butts
could not feel that slid anymore

We use to dangle from that monkey bar
until our little arms
were too tired to hold on any longer

We use to work that
playground

Work it like the hooker
down on Madison Street
worked her corner

Work it like Jesses
use to work that whiskey bottle
until every last drop was gone

We would work that playground
until the sky was dark
until our mamas called us
to come home

Last time I saw that playground
it was rusty and cranky
with weeds growing through cement
and just plain tired
like a worn out old man

When Aintee Beverly Calls

now there are those who will not call

to spoil your otherwise day
even if they should reveal
but their heart can not find a way

and sorrows don't go down easy
makes you weak and feeling all alone
the deeper the hole you have fallen in
the longer the pain will hold on

when aunt Beverly calls
leaves a message in a voicemail
with no specifics to say
you better hold on
you better hold on
its gonna be a bad day

when aunt Beverly calls
leaves a message in a voicemail
with no specifics to say
you better hold on
you better hold on
its gonna be a bad day

now cousin Bernice she is strange
delivers bad news with a happy smile
which takes the long way to your heart oh yeah
and then it hits you like running a quarter mile

and sorrows don't go down easy
makes you weak and feeling all alone
the deeper the hole you have fallen in
the longer the pain will hold on

when aunt Beverly calls
leaves a message in a voicemail
with no specifics to say
you better hold on
its gonna be a bad day

My Stuff

I use to have stuff
Lots of stuff

Stuff that I wore
proudly
Stuff that I carried around
in my pocket stuff
Stuff that I would
place in places
among other stuff
to be seen
by others who
probably had their
own stuff

I really loved
my stuff

Now I can not even
find my stuff
I have gone through
so much stuff
only to find
the new stuff

I keep asking myself
where is my stuff?
Stuff just don't get up
and run off, does it?

Once I saw my stuff
in the home
of somebody else
next to their stuff
I thought for a second
but I let that stuff go

I am now taking photos
of all my new stuff
and placing it on
one of those shared sites
so at least I can connect
with stuff that might
go missing

If anyone listening
holding on
to my stuff
please have pity
and return my stuff

I really miss my stuff

You See OJ

Motivated by passion
Once told a beautiful girl
I could touch the ceiling
She said not in this world

I made a wager
that she thought through
and finally agreed
to allow me to be a fool

I had never done such a thing
and no reason to jump that high
but I was drivin by passion
Ready and willing to give it a try

I jump out of my shoes
thought I would never come down
I smacked that ceiling for good measure
so she could hear my victory sound

Restvale Cemetery

stealing from our love ones
dug up graves
the care keepers did
searching for valuable to spend
sounded much like crack heads
who ever though that door
was opened
to allow those fools in
or just bad people
and Chicago has their share
disrespecting what was sacred
breaking hearts once again
even while love one resting
after lives that were met by violence
to end their journey
can't catch a break and just can't win
Notables include
Ezzard Charles world heavyweight boxing champion
Big Walter Horton American blues harmonica player
Otis Spann blues pianist
Emmett Till death helped galvanize
the U.S. Civil Rights Movement
and there was
Dinah Washington "Queen of the Blues"

NO WAY

not going backwards
the struggle was too hard
losing many far greater
that he could never
measure up to

when this nightmare
is over
his life will be a lesson
much like touching fire
for the first time

protest his businesses
the thought of a library
so disheartening
as he has shown such disrespect

LIBERAL

I am a liberal
which means that I will help you
when you are down
and nothing else
I desire to live around liberals
like myself
who care about people first
the environment
the future
I prefer to talk among liberals
Send my children to schools taught by liberals
Work for liberals
Spend my money among liberals
I thank my creator for giving me
the wisdom
to be the best liberal
I can be

Bob Moore

I have written around 2000 song lyrics, both completed and parts. Some turned into children books, poems, plays, and even art. I got lucky with some, while at the other end, I found many embarrassing and wondered if they came from me and why. Like the "99 Cent Man," but this raw Texan liked it and so I put it out. Different strokes for different folks, as the saying goes. I am sure it could have been a Reggae or even a Tony Bennett like presentation. The most important point was my late friend and mentor Bob Moore, back in the Fiji Islands, who I shared my first song lyrics with at his takeaway on Grantham Road in a place call Rawai, Fiji Islands. He probably lied to me by saying it was very good, complete with the gyrations as he shakes his head while fanning himself to catch some evening breeze. I ran with that because that is what I wanted to hear. A lesson learned. Never burst somebody's private bubble. Inspire and they will go away and come back with more. Like it or not.Especially children, but we all need stroking, and so say something nice and encouraging, and especially with children. So, 2000 songs later, all the thanks Bob and rest in peace my friend because I have some more for you.

N Word

I never got over the Chicago Police as a child. First time I heard the "N" word at age 3 or 4 but did not know what it meant, but I knew it was used in conjunction with a night stick on Madison and Levitt. No one was using that word in the home or in the streets, unless it was after my bedtime. We were running away from that word by fleeing Mississippi. That is why there is such a generation gap today over that word. Young people do not respect the struggle, not until they get harassed and locked up. If the struggle is not in a movie with a dope soundtrack, they will not know because they do not read, at least mines don't. If you asked them who John Lewis is, they would embarrass you. You never heard the "N" used during Arethas' services. Why? Because it is offensive but the driving forces behind some of the music and they are corporations, they let it slide just as long as it impacts our young people to keep them null and void.

A Man

saw the struggles
with some passed on to me
but I can not speak well
because I am not a woman

saw the relationships
with some with violence
but I can not speak well
because I am not a woman

saw things that I would not do
ever in my lifetime
and that I can speak well
it is my responsibility
because I am a man

I AM EVERYTHING BAD

That evening after the OJ chase
found myself in an LA supermarket
with all eyes upon me
as if I was going to rob the store
Robbery is not in my resume
feeling uncomfortable at the checkout
as they kept on staring
and I want leave cannot take any more

Right after 9/11 at the Dallas Airport
checkin lady staring me down
alerting white people to do the same
Feeling angry but I cannot show that
but I got something for this broad
I had my government employee ID
but this heffer disrespected my position
Sent me to max security
to remind me where I am at

In Memory of

Mother Alberta
Sister Juanita
Cousin Roger Smith
Cousin Bernard Hayes
Cousin Tanya Hates
and
friend and mentor Bob Moore

Thanks to Pixibay for use of image